Galloway's
Marathon FAQ

Jeff Galloway

Galloway's Marathon FAQ

Over 100 of the most frequently asked questions

Meyer & Meyer Sport

British Library Cataloguing in Publication Data
A catalogue record for this book is available from the British Library

Jeff Galloway: Galloway's Marathon FAQ
Maidenhead: Meyer & Meyer Sport (UK) Ltd., 2009
ISBN 978-1-84126-266-6

© 2009 by Meyer & Meyer Sport (UK) Ltd.
Adelaide, Auckland, Budapest, Cape Town, Graz, Indianapolis,
Maidenhead, Olten (CH), Singapore, Toronto
Member of the World
Sport Publishers' Association (WSPA)
www.w-s-p-a.org
Printed and bound by: B.O.S.S Druck und Medien GmbH, Germany
ISBN 978-1-84126-266-6
E-Mail: info@m-m-sports.com
www.m-m-sports.com

Contents

SECTION 1:
General Questions

Question
What is so special about finishing a marathon?

Answer

Thousands of runners, many who have been high achievers in their career, have told me that finishing a marathon gave them the greatest sense of accomplishment and achievement ever. Not only do you have to put together 4-6 months of hard training, but during every long run and the race itself, each person has to draw upon resources inside. The empowerment gained from completing this journey often leads to other positive life changes.

Question

What are the three crucial training elements needed for finishing a marathon with strength?

Answer

1. A very slow long run that gradually increases to 26 miles or more (using strategic walk breaks).

2. Two 30 minute "maintenance" runs during the week-usually on Tuesday and Thursday.

3. Days off from running-especially the day before the long run. Note: Pacing and schedules are detailed in the book RUNNING – A YEAR ROUND PLAN.

Question

Can anyone finish a marathon?

Answer

I've heard from well over ten thousand runners, including many in their 60's and 70's, who take their first running steps in our Galloway program and finish a marathon within 9 months. Those who could not run around the block have used the Galloway program to finish with strength without injury. Almost anyone can finish a marathon if they 1) go slowly enough on the long runs, 2) gradually build the distance of the long one close to 26 miles, and 3) use the correct run-walk-run ratio, according to my experience.

Question
What are the training components needed to run a faster time in the marathon?

Answer

1. A very slow long run that increases to 29 miles, three to four weeks before the marathon.

2. A series of mile repeat workouts done on some of the non-long-run weekends increasing to a maximum of 14 x 1 mile.

3. A few running form drills done each week, during the short runs.

4. Strategic rest days that allow for rebuilding after the hard workouts.

Note:

The training is detailed in my book RUNNING – A YEAR ROUND PLAN.

Question
What effect does age have on a marathon training program?

Answer

In researching this issue for my book RUNNING UNTIL YOU'RE 100, I found quite a few runners above the age of 70 who run many marathons. Most told me that they had no orthopedic problems – even those who were running their 26.2-mile events every other weekend. I've found it best to add extra rest days with each additional decade, and increase the frequency of walk breaks as detailed in this book. There is also a section on age adjustments in my book RUNNING – A YEAR ROUND PLAN.

Question

How can I tell how fast I'm capable of running?

Answer

I've designed a "magic mile" time trial that can very accurately predict what your maximum performance would be during a given season. About every 3 weeks, in the middle of a shorter distance workout, run one measured mile for time. For details on this accurate predictor, see the TRAINING section in this book.

Question
Doesn't marathon training force you to deal with pain?

Answer

Debilitating aches, pains, and fatigue are what I call 'self-imposed punishment.' While it is common to have a few minor aches or pains as the long run distance increases, most of these go away within 2-3 days IF 1) the pacing is slow enough, 2) the run-walk-run ratio is conservative enough, and 3) there is a rest day (no running) between runs.

Question

THE MAGIC INGREDIENT: Tell me one marathon training change that will make me feel good when I run and finish with strength?

Answer

The use of my run-walk-run method will do this. Inserting walk breaks frequently enough, from the beginning of training runs and the race itself, gives each runner control over tiredness. The same endurance is gained from a liberal run-walk-run strategy as when running continuously. With each walk break, the muscle can rebound and recover, while fatigue is erased. Walk breaks allow you to push the endurance "wall" farther and farther. See the run-walk-run section of this book and RUNNING – A YEAR ROUND PLAN for details.

Question
How do you choose a group to train with?

Answer

Group support can increase motivation and fun during the long runs. It is crucial that the pace of the group be slow enough for the slowest member (two minutes per mile slower than current marathon race pace). The most successful programs tend to subdivide into pace groups based upon an evaluation of current pace potential, with each group led by a group leader who ensures a slow pace for each. I've found that the use of the correct run-walk-run ratio reduces aches and pains and allows one to carry on other life activities after the long runs.

Question
How do you find a training group?

Answer

Visit

www.RunInjuryFree.com

and other running websites to see if there is a group in your area. Some running stores will either offer group training, or have contact information for groups in your area.

Question

What is the history of the marathon?

Answer

The longest races in the ancient Olympics were approximately five thousand meters (3.1 miles). The idea for the marathon race came from Pierre de Coubertin, founder of the modern Olympic Games (1896). As a young history student, Pierre was impressed with the story of the messenger Phidippides who fought in the battle of Marathon (490 BC), ran the news of the Athenian victory to Athens, and died after delivering the message (according to legend). According to experts, the route of the first Olympic Marathon race was the route used by Phidippides. The marathon is only one of two events that have been run in every edition of the modern games.

Question
Why do we run 26.2 miles?

Answer

The first race, from the battle site into the 1896 Olympic stadium, was determined to be 40 kilometers, or 25 miles. In 1908, the Olympics were held in London and the route was charted to start 40K outside Olympic Stadium, as in Athens. When the queen asked to have the course extended to start at Windsor Palace, the organizers agreed. The 26.2 – mile distance of the new course became the Olympic standard. So when you pass the 25-mile mark and wish the race was finished, you can say "God save the Queen" (or something similar). But the distance is quite legitimate. Phidippides would not have stopped at the site of the 1896 stadium, but would have continued into the ancient town of Athens. The total distance would be about the currently certified distance.

SECTION 2: TROUBLESHOOTING PROBLEMS, WITH SOLUTIONS

Question

Why do I slow down at a certain point (usually 20 miles) in the marathon?

Is this "The Wall?"

Answer

"The Wall" is the point where the leg muscles acquire such a level of fatigue that they don't work very well. Runners often reach this state very suddenly. One can expect this to occur within a mile or so of the longest distance run in the past 4 weeks. For example, if you have run 20 miles as your longest run, you can expect to get very tired and slow down after you pass this mileage point in the marathon itself. The wall can avoided by 1) increasing the length of the long run to at least 26 miles, 3-4 weeks before race day, 2) slowing your pace during the first part of the race, and 3) inserting walk breaks more frequently from mile 1 until mile 20 or so during the marathon. Note: Time goal runners will find successful pacing and training schedules to their goals in my book RUNNING – A YEAR ROUND PLAN.

Question
How do I know that I've hit "The Wall?"

Answer

When paced correctly, fatigue creeps up on you, gradually. Unfortunately, there are no clear-cut signs that you are about to encounter "The Wall" until you are there. This often happens within the length of a football field. You're feeling tired but confident of finishing and within a few yards feel suddenly exhausted. The muscles don't work the way they did a few minutes before. The only running form that can work is a "shuffling" mode in which the feet are next to the ground, touching lightly, with a short stride.

Question
I get light-headed, and have trouble concentrating at the end of my long runs.

Answer

In investigating this condition among my runners, I've discovered that the most common reason for this is low blood sugar. In this case, increasing the blood sugar snacks, such as gel products or candy, can provide psychological relief. The general rule of thumb is to consume 30-40 calories per mile, with 2-4 oz of water, every 1-2 miles. Most find that they need to start taking the blood sugar boosters about 4-6 miles into a long run.

Some of the light-headedness is due to fatigue. By taking walk breaks often enough from the beginning and starting more slowly, this problem can often be managed or eliminated.

Question
Can I continue to run when injured?

Answer

Most injuries will allow for some running – if you take about a week off to get the healing started you stay below the threshold of irritation. These factors will help you do this:

1. gentle walking for the first 5 minutes and then liberal use of walk breaks,

2. running at a pace slow enough so that you don't aggravate the injured area,

3. maintain a short stride with feet low to the ground, and

4. stopping the run before you have aggravated the injury. Be sure to get your doctor's OK before you run when injured.

Question
My back gets sore or hurts.

Answer

A forward lean often causes this. Run like a "puppet on a string," especially coming out of each walk break: head is over shoulders, over the hips, as the foot touches underneath.

When the stride is slightly too long, the twisting motion of the hips/back can sometimes result in a sore back. The most important time to reduce stride length is during the second half of a run – particularly a long run.

Question
The front of my shins hurt.

Answer

Shorten your stride – especially at the end of a long run. Avoid running fast (for you) to stay below the threshold of irritation so it can heal.

Question
My feet hurt.

Answer

Make sure you have enough cushion in your shoe and the insole under your foot. It helps to get a "shoe check" with a really experienced running store staff member. If pain persists, see a podiatrist who has treated a lot of runners for the same problem.

Question

I will be running a marathon but did not get up to 26-mile distance on the last long run.

What is the best way to be strong at the end of the race?

Answer

For example, if your longest run, 3 weeks before the marathon was 18 miles, you need to walk for the first 6-8 miles and then use the run-walk-run ratio that worked for you on the last long run (better to add more walking). Option 2: If you ran 3 minutes/walked 1 minute during your last long one, you should be fine in the marathon using a 1-1 from the beginning. The running pace should also be reduced.

Question

I missed one of my long runs. What should I do?

Answer

Most can catch up with the marathon training schedule in my books (such as RUNNING – A YEAR ROUND PLAN) by walking the extra distance needed before the next long run. For example, on the next one, walk for the first 5-6 miles, and then use a more conservative run-walk-run strategy than you would normally use. It is also possible to dramatically increase the amount of walking, from the beginning of the run. For example, if you have been running 3 minutes/walking 1 minute, drop back to run 1 minute/walk 1 minute. If you have been using a 1-1, then run 20 seconds/walk 40 seconds.

Question
I can't run outside.

Answer

Treadmill runs are suitable substitutes for short runs outdoors. The downside is that you will not simulate the adaptations that feet make with the road, and the adjustments to outside weather conditions. Long runs should be done on the type of surface used in the race itself, if at all possible. If you must run most of the long run on a treadmill, try to run at least the last 25% of the long run on the marathon race surface.

Question
What is the best warm-up?

Answer

The concept is to gently introduce the feet and legs to the running motion. Walk for 2 minutes very gently, then walk for 2-3 minutes at a relaxed and natural pace (no power walking). For the next 10 minutes, start running in shorter segments than you plan to do later in the run. For example, if you plan to run for 3 minutes and walk for a minute, begin by running for a minute and walking for a minute (or 30 seconds/30 seconds).

Question
What is the best cross-training for a marathon?

Answer

Water running is the only cross-training mode that I've found which may improve your running. This can be done on a non-running day, as a second workout on a running day, or can even serve as a substitute for a short run (Tues/Thurs).

Question

How do I ease off (taper down) on training leading up to the marathon?

Answer

The last long run is scheduled 3-4 weeks before the race. First time marathoners cannot improve their conditioning during this period, so maintenance running is all that is needed: slow runs of 30 minutes, on Tuesday and Thursday. On the weekends, the distance of the runs only needs to be 6-7 miles.

Two weeks before the goal marathon, experienced marathoners with time goals have one more improvement component that can help: a 14 x 1 mile speed workout. It's best to run very easily on the other running days – especially during the last two weeks.

I hear about dozens of injuries, every marathon season, from runners who get a bit too excited during the last two weeks and run too fast or too far. It is always better to do the minimum during the last 14 days.

Question
Can I exercise the day before long runs/marathons?

Answer

It's best to avoid running and to take it very easy the day before a long run, and on the day of the marathon itself. Walking around for 30-60 minutes should be fine. This is what most marathoners do at the race expo, the day before the marathon.

Question
Can I run a race as a long run?

Answer

If you can run slowly enough, and take the required walk breaks, it's OK to use a race as a long run. But it's hard for most runners to go slowly enough in the beginning of a race. The excitement and the constant flow of other runners often results in a pace that is a few seconds per mile too fast. This can compromise the training program due to increased risk of injury and lingering fatigue. If you plan to do this, start at the back of the pack. This will give you more freedom to take the assigned walk breaks, and keep the pace slow – at least in the beginning. Remember that you cannot run too slow or take too many walk breaks on long training runs.

Question
I get nauseous when I eat before a run.

Answer

Most runners don't need to eat anything before a run. Diabetics and those with severe blood sugar issues may need to consume a small quantity of 30-40 calories, within 30 minutes of the start of a run. Practice eating before long runs so that you know what types of foods won't cause problems, how much to eat, and when to eat.

Question

My running friend runs faster than I run.

When I try to keep up, I get extremely tired or injured.

Answer

Talk to your friend about this. It will not hurt a faster runner to slow down on long runs. But running too fast, as the distance increases, is a major source of injury. If the friend will not slow down, you can run the short runs with him or her. This will give you a speed workout.

Note:

For more injury suggestions, see the injury section of the book.

SECTION 3: TRAINING

Question
How far should my longest long run be?

Answer

To finish with strength, I've found it best to build the long one up to 26 miles, 3-4 weeks before race day. For marathon time improvement, 29 miles is recommended.

Question
Can a longer long run help me run faster in my marathon?

Answer

In several surveys, I've found that those who used to run 20 miles as their farthest training distance, improved by an average of more than 15 minutes when they boosted the last long run to 26 miles. Further research showed that those who ran 26 miles in previous training programs achieved an average of 11 minutes of time improvement by increasing long run distance to 29 miles.

Question
How often should the long run be run?

Answer

When the length of the run is 9 miles or less, you can run every week or every other week as long as you are running slowly enough (see question on long run pacing). It is better for most runners to run long every other week, covering one third to one half of the distance on the non-long-run weekends. When the long run reaches 10 miles, run the long one every other week, with a 3-5 mile run on the alternate weekend. At 17-mile long run distance, it's best to run long every 3rd weekend. When the distance of the long run reaches 26 miles, you can run long every 3rd or 4th weekend.

Question

How much should I run on the two short mileage days each week?

Answer

You only need to run two 30-minute runs, two days a week (usually Tues and Thurs) to maintain the endurance gained on the longer weekend runs. These shorter runs can be run at whatever pace you wish using the run-walk-run ratio of your choice. You may eliminate the walk breaks on these short runs, if you're not experiencing aches, pains and longer recovery issues.

Question
Should I take walk breaks on the short mileage days?

Answer

You may opt to take no walk breaks on these "maintenance" days, if you don't have problems due to aches, pains and longer recovery from running continuously.

Question
What if I want to run more days per week?

Answer

It is OK to do this, provided you are recovering well from the weekend runs. My YEAR ROUND PLAN book schedules 3 running days other than the weekend run – with various training elements scattered throughout, and I've not seen any injuries related to running 4 days a week. Every additional day beyond 4, however, increases injury risk due to lack of recovery from the harder workouts.

Question
How long should I run on the non-long-run weekends?

Answer
During the first 2 months of the program, when the long runs are less than 12 miles, the minimum distance is 3 miles. After that, the minimum would be 25% of the current long run distance, during the shorter weekend runs.

Question
What if I want to run longer on the non-long-run weekends?

Answer
As long as you are recovering quickly between long runs, you can run longer on these days. It is best to run no more than 10 miles on these lower mileage weekends. It is doubtful that longer runs on these "recovery weekends" will help you run faster or improve conditioning in any way.

Question
If the body is strong and recovering well, can't I eliminate rest days?

Answer

This is not a good idea. During the rest days, the body rebuilds stronger. The increased distance of the long run produces the endurance needed for completing the marathon, without injury, if the pace is appropriate and there is sufficient rest before and after each long run. In other words, the hard work on long runs and speed sessions will not produce better conditioning unless there is enough rest for the running muscles, on the rest days.

Question
What is the meaning of "junk miles?"

Answer

Running a few miles, on a day that should be a rest day, will not improve conditioning. But even a few miles may interfere with the recovery of the muscles, tendons, joints and feet. When you are continuing to increase workload, as in a marathon, injury risk goes down when you don't run on a rest day. You could do cross-training that does not use the calf muscle.

Question
How much rest is needed after a speed workout?

Answer

Time goal runners will do mile repeat speed workouts to build speed. But if there is not enough rest between these stress workouts, the body will not rebuild and often breaks down with injury. Alternating running days with rest or walking days has been a great way to allow for rebuilding while maintaining current fitness.

Question

How many days per week do I need to run to finish a marathon?

Answer

Only three days a week are needed. The long run is usually done on the weekend. On two other days (usually Tuesday and Thursday) you'll only need to run for 30 minutes as maintenance for finishing the marathon.

Question
How many miles per week?

Answer

Weekly mileage is not important. I've experienced an over 98% success rate in my Galloway Training Programs with an average mileage of only about 13 miles a week. The crucial element in finishing is the progressive increase of the long run to 26 miles, 3-4 weeks before the marathon.

Question

How do I know what pace to run in long runs and in the race itself?

Answer

Read the response to the next question, concerning the "magic mile." This simple time trial has been the best method I've found to accurately predict what you are capable of running on a perfect day, but will also tell what is a safe pace for long runs. Be sure to read the adjustments to be made for temperature and other factors.

Question
What is the "Magic Mile" time trial?

Answer

This one-mile time trial has been shown to very accurately predict current maximum potential in the marathon. It is placed into the training schedule (see RUNNING – A YEAR ROUND PLAN schedules) about every 3 weeks. The first one should not be all-out – just a little faster than you have been running. On each successive trial, your goal is to beat the previous best time. After about 4 of these, most runners are going about as fast as they can currently run for a mile. By using the formula listed in the next answer, one can accurately predict current performance.

Question

How much do I slow down from my magic mile pace?

Answer

After analyzing the data from thousands of performances, I've discovered that runners run about 30% slower during a marathon, compared with their time on a fast one mile by itself. So take your fastest one-mile time and multiply by 1.3. This predicts the fastest performance you can expect, 1) on an ideal day with no crowds, 2) after having done all of the training listed in my training program (speedwork and long runs up to 29 miles), and 3) without challenges on the course, hills, infections, etc. This is an extreme effort and so I recommend slowing this pace down by 20 seconds/mile at least, for the first 5 miles, to adjust for non-ideal factors. This allows you to control the level of exertion desired in your marathon race.

Question
How fast should I run during my long runs?

Answer

I recommend pacing all of the long runs, at least two minutes per mile slower than predicted by the magic mile, adjusted for heat. I've not found any pace that is too slow. You'll receive the endurance based upon the distance of the current long run. In other words, a long run at 20 minutes per mile for 15 miles gives the same endurance as a 15 - mile run at 10 minutes per mile or at 5 minutes per mile.

Take the magic mile time, multiply by 1.3 and add two minutes. Finally, slow down according to a temperature increase, as noted below. It is better to slow down even further. Even a pace that is 4-5 minutes per mile slower than goal pace has produced the same endurance as a faster paced training run.

Slow the long run pace as the temperature increases, as follows:
30 seconds a mile slower for every 5°F temperature increase above 60°F
20 seconds per kilometer slower for every 2°C above 15°C.

Example on the next page…

Example

10:00 on the magic mile
x 1.3 = 13 min per mile (really hard marathon pace)
plus 2 min = 15 min/mi long run training pace
At 70°F: 16 min/mi
At 80°F: 17 min/mi

At 14°C or cooler: 8:04 per km
At 18°C: 8:44 per km
At 22°C: 9:24 per km
It is always better to run slower on the long runs.

Note

There is a pace calculator, based upon the magic mile, on our website:

www.JeffGalloway.com

Question
How fast should I run during my first marathon?

Answer

For the first 18 miles of the first marathon, pace yourself as if you were running a long run: at least two minutes per mile slower than that predicted by the magic mile, adjusted for temperature. The run-walk-run strategy would be adjusted for pace. After 18 miles, if you're feeling strong, you can pick up the pace, and reduce the walk breaks. The example in the answer above can guide you to a normally safe training pace, with temperature adjustments.

Question

If I have run a marathon before, have run a 29 mile long run and done all of the speedwork, can I start the race at the predicted race pace (magic mile x 1.3)?

Answer

Even when you've done your homework, it is still a good idea to start a bit slower than goal pace. Since most of my runners achieve their fastest times when running the second half faster than the first half, I recommend slowing by 10-20 seconds per mile for the first 5-6 miles. If all is well, ease down to goal pace until mile 18. At that point you can hold pace or speed up if you feel strong.

This assumes ideal weather conditions (60°F or 15°C or cooler), no crowds, and that you have done all of the long runs and speed sessions recommended in my book RUNNING – A YEAR ROUND PLAN.

Question
Why run so slow on long runs?

Answer

I've not found any pace that is too slow. Long run endurance is gained by the distance covered: 20 min/mi pace gives the same endurance as 5 min/mi pace. Running too fast during a long run, however, has been the most common cause of injury or slower recovery, based upon my coaching experience. Since there is no benefit from running faster and there are a lot of problems when doing so, I suggest following the guidelines noted in the previous question.

Question

What pace should I run on the short days during the week?

Answer

As long as you have no aches, pains or injuries, you can choose the pace for your short days. Injury risk is reduced with a slow pace, with frequent walk breaks. But experienced runners who like to run faster can do so if there are no signs that this interferes with recovery.

SECTION 4:
NUTRITION FOR
TRAINING AND
RACING

Question
How much should I eat the day before a long run?

Answer

On the day before your long runs, practice eating. Be sure to jot down what you eat, and how much. You can fine-tune the plan as you go through the program, based upon what works for you. Then, on the day before your marathon, you will replicate the eating routine that works for you. In my book RUNNING – A YEAR ROUND PLAN, you'll find a successful eating plan, but you should adjust it to your needs. Here are the general rules:

1. Don't eat a large meal after 5pm the afternoon before.

2. Avoid salty food and alcohol the afternoon and evening before long runs and the race.

3. Eat smaller meals or snacks about every 2-3 hours, starting about 12 noon the day before.

4. Choose foods that digest easily.

5. Drink 6-8 oz of water or sports drink with your snacks.

6. It takes about 36-48 hours for the food you eat to be digested, metabolized and ready to be used in the muscles during exercise. Last minute nutrition "cramming" will not help you during the run.

7. I've never seen a runner die of starvation during a marathon.

Question
What should I drink the day before long runs?

Answer

Drink about 6-8 oz of water or sports drink, about every 2-3 hours. Accelerade has been shown by good research to help normalize your fluid levels better than water and another sports drink. I recommend a total of 50-64 oz of fluid throughout the day. Avoid alcohol!

Question
What should I eat and drink before the race?

Answer

The eating/drinking strategy that works for you, before long runs, should be your guide. Fine-tune the amount and the timing and use the pattern that works best. Unless you are diabetic or have severe blood sugar problems, you may not need to eat anything at all. If you get nausea from eating before running, reduce the amount or don't eat at all before long runs, and see how this works. Most of the runners I've worked with, who do not eat breakfast, start their blood sugar intake at 2-3 miles into the run. I recommend taking 6-8 oz of water, about 2-3 hours before the start. Practice this before long runs so that you will visit the toilet before the start-especially if you drink coffee. Coffee has actually been shown to improve endurance and enhance fat-burning, but you need to find the right timetable for consumption.

Question
What should I eat during long runs and the race itself?

Answer

Running a marathon puts enough stress on the system to shut down the digestive tract. Therefore, very little of the food and fluid you consume during a run can be used during that run. It is possible to absorb a small amount of fluid, and blood sugar booster, every 15 minutes or so, and this can help you stay motivated. Your brain needs glycogen as fuel. As you continue, mile after mile on long runs, the available supply of this limited resource is reduced. If you don't consume enough to boost the blood glucose (using gel products, hard candies, gummy bears, energy bars) the mental focus and motivation is reduced. You can maintain mental energy and avoid some of the negative messages at the end of your race by eating small amounts of foods with sugar, regularly. Practice taking several products during long runs to find what works best for you. This allows each runner to discover the best source, the amount, the quantity of water, the frequency, and how to adjust as the distance increases. A rule of thumb, based upon the runners I've worked with, is the following: 30-40 calories every 1-2 miles, starting with mile 5. Be sure to drink a little water with each blood sugar snack.

Question
What should I eat, and when, after a long run or speed workout?

Answer

The 30-minute period after a long or hard workout is prime time for reloading your needed glycogen supply. This is very important for recovery because glycogen is the exclusive fuel source needed during the first 15 minutes of exercise, and is the brain's source of energy. If you miss the first half hour, you can still reload the storage areas during the next 60 minutes, but this is not quite as good for reloading. I recommend a snack of 200-300 calories that is composed of 80% simple carbohydrate and 20% protein. Research has confirmed that this combination can help reload your storage more effectively.

SECTION 5:
THE RUN-WALK-RUN METHOD

Question

Why does the run-walk-run method produce faster race times and speed up recovery?

Answer

After hearing from hundreds of thousands of runners who have tried it both ways, almost every single runner who has used the right run-walk-run strategy (based upon pace) has experienced benefits. The average time improvement, under similar conditions, among those who used to run continuously is more than 13 minutes faster when using the correct ratio of walk breaks.

Question
What is the principle behind the run-walk-run method?

Answer

This is a form of interval training and is directly tied to the conservation of resources: muscle, feet, joints, energy, fluids, etc. The continuous use of the running muscles will produce fatigue much more quickly. By inserting walk breaks as early and as often as needed, you can erase most of the fatigue with each walk break. The muscle and energy resources you conserve early will allow you to feel strong at the end of the run, and speed up the recovery.

Question
How do walk breaks prevent injury?

Answer

Running continuously will increase the fatigue significantly in muscles, tendons, joints, etc. Without having a break from constant use, wear patterns develop in specific areas. Some of these sites become "weak links" which get inflamed or injured. When walk breaks are taken from the beginning of the run, stress is released from working muscles and the stress on the weak links is reduced significantly. Some restoration can occur in worn areas – even during a run – when walk breaks are taken often enough. When an individual adjusts the run-walk-run ratios conservatively enough, the stress on the weak links doesn't accumulate to a level that produces significant damage. So each element in the system (bones, muscles, tendons, joints) can adapt and improve during the recovery after each long run. If the run-walk-run ratio is conservative enough, even the damage from a 26-mile run is minimal and can be repaired relatively quickly.

Question
How can I run faster with walk breaks?

Answer

According to several surveys, those who used to run continuously in marathons improved an average of more than 13 minutes when they shifted to my run-walk-run method. By taking the walks early, the muscles stay strong and are ready for the challenge later. Because the walk breaks erase most of the fatigue, you don't slow down during the last 6-8 miles in the marathon, and many of our folks increase pace at the end. So instead of slowing down 9-15 minutes during the last 8 miles, walk breakers stay on pace or speed up. By using the method, you can be the one who is passing people at the end, celebrating afterward.

Question
How can I make up the time I lose during a walk break?

Answer

One of the great surprises from the walk break experience is how naturally you catch up with the runners who don't walk, during the running segments. Try this: notice one or two people who are running near you or just ahead when you start your walk break. You will drop behind during a walk break by a few yards. But if you are using the right strategy and pace, each walk restores the strength and capacity of the muscles so that you find yourself catching up during the running portion. Be prepared to pick new "markers" during the second half of the marathon: Those who don't take the walk breaks will start slipping behind you.

Question

How much faster will I have to run during my running segments, when I take a walk break?

Answer

This depends upon a lot of individual factors, especially the pace of the walk. In numerous surveys, we've found that most runners lose 10-20 seconds when they take a one-minute walk break. Let's say that a runner has a goal pace of 10 minutes per mile. The standard run-walk-run strategy at this pace is (run 3 minutes/walk 1 minute).

Most of the runners I've monitored at 10 min/mi pace tend to lose about 15 seconds when they walk for one minute. This means that for every minute run, the runner only has to run 5 seconds faster. This has been very easy to do for the runners that I've worked with, when the pace is right, for the person, on that day.

Question
How often should I take walk breaks?

Answer

Walk breaks are directly connected to the pace that is being run at that time. Here are the most successful strategies based upon my experience:

7 min/mi-run 1 mile, walk 30-45 seconds
7:30/mi-run 5 minutes, walk 30-45 seconds
8:00/mi-run 4 minutes, walk 30 seconds
8:30/mi-run 4 minutes, walk 45 seconds
9:00/mi-run 4 minutes, walk 1 minute (4-1)
10:00/mi-run 3 minutes, walk 1 minute
11:00/mi-2:30-1
12:00/mi-2-1
13:00/mi-1-1
14:00/mi-30 seconds-30 seconds
15:00/mi-30 seconds run-45 seconds walk
16:00/mi-20 sec run-40 sec walk
17:00/mi-15 sec run-45 sec walk
18:00/mi-10 sec run-50 sec walk

Note:

It is always OK to take more frequent walk breaks than listed.

Question
Do I have to take walk breaks at the beginning of my run?

Answer

The most effective walk breaks are those taken at the beginning of the run. With correct pacing, the walk breaks taken at the beginning of the run can erase all of the fatigue to that point. If you wait to take the walk breaks, you will accumulate fatigue that may not be erased that day.

Question

If I haven't used walk breaks in training, should I take them in a race?

Answer

Yes! This is one of the few exceptions to the rule "don't try anything new in the marathon that you haven't used in training." The walk breaks save your muscle resources, fuel, feet, and joints. I've now heard from thousands who tried my run-walk-run method for the first time in a race and experienced success in a range of ways. Even if you use the run-walk-run for the first half of a marathon, try it.

Question

Should I move to the side of the road to take my walk breaks?

Answer

Yes. Both sides of the road are appropriate areas for taking walk breaks. Either stay on one side of the road or move over before walking. If you sense that the runners behind you are too close or the crowd is too thick, it helps to verbally warn the other runners by saying something like "walk break in 5 seconds, 4, 3, 2, 1."

Question

What if I reach a point in the run where it's hard to start running again?

Answer

Most of the runners I've heard from who have had this problem, did not take the walk breaks often enough in the beginning of their run. If you are having trouble re-starting your run, use the "shuffle" instead of walking. Shuffling is simply keeping your feet right next to the ground, shortening stride, and maintaining a motion that is a combination of walking and running. The effort level is less that running but the pace is not much slower. Some folks just continue shuffling with a few running breaks during the rest of the run.

Question
What happens mentally when you take walk breaks?

Answer

When the walk breaks are short enough for you on that day, you'll eliminate much of the mental stress due to fatigue and the stress of too many "more miles to go." You only need to focus on the amount of running during a run segment. If that amount is challenging, reduce it. This gives you control over your fatigue—and empowers you to keep going, one segment at a time. So if you are using a 1-1 ratio, you don't have think "I have 20 miles to go." Your only mission is "one more minute."

Question
How fast should I walk?

Answer

Since the purpose of the walk break is to erase fatigue, it's best to walk slowly enough for this to occur. Most of my running clients walk at a comfortable pace. Above all, keep the stride length short enough so that you are not stressing the hamstring, the tendon behind the knee or the anterior tibial muscle on the front of the shin. It is usually OK to speed up the walk by increasing turnover of the legs when walking – with a short stride.

SECTION 6: TRAINING TO FINISH

Question
How many training days per week are necessary?

Answer

The minimum is three running days per week. In fact, the "three day a week" runners experience the lowest rate of injury. When runners increase the number of running days, they usually suffer more aches, pains and injuries. The long runs build the endurance necessary to finish. The two additional training days simply maintain conditioning.

Question

How far and how fast should one go on the two maintenance runs?

Answer

A 30-minute minimum is needed. You can run at any speed, using any run-walk-run ratio desired, on these runs. It is OK to run faster on these runs, if you're recovering well from the weekend workouts. You may reduce the number of walk breaks or eliminate them on these short runs, if you are not having problems with aches, pains or lingering fatigue.

Question
How long should the long run be?

Answer

To finish with strength, it's best to build up to a long run of at least 26 miles. To maximize time improvement, I recommend that the last long one be 29 miles. I've found it best to schedule the last long one 3-4 weeks before marathon race day. These long ones should be run very slowly as noted in the answer to the question on long run pacing. There is also a lot of information in my books RUNNING – A YEAR ROUND PLAN, & GALLOWAY TRAINING PROGRAMS.

Question

Can a longer long run help me improve my time in the marathon?

Answer

In several surveys, I've found that those who step up from a longest run of 20 miles or less to our recommended 26 – miler, experience an average improvement of more than 15 minutes. Those who go from a 26 – miler one season, to a longest of 29 miles in a later training program, run an average of 11 minutes faster in the marathon under comparable conditions.

Question
What about alternative exercise on the off days?

Answer

The schedules I offer in my training books are the minimum that has allowed the runners I've coached to achieve their goals. Alternative or cross-training exercises can be done on the days when there is not a run scheduled. Most of these exercises will not help or hurt running performance. Water running is the only cross-training mode that I believe improves running form and performance. Avoid stair machines, spinning, and high impact aerobics on days that should be "off" days from running.

Question

Can I run longer on the short, maintenance days?

Answer

As long as you are not having aches, pains or injuries when you increase the short run distance, you can add to the distance on those short days. Based upon my experience, I don't believe that the extra distance will improve marathon performance.

Question

How fast should I try to run my first marathon?

Answer

The magic mile (MM) will tell you about your current capabilities by predicting a current all-out pace under ideal conditions. I recommend running all of the training runs, and the first 20 miles of the marathon at a pace that is 2 min/mi slower than predicted by the MM – with adjustments for weather. (30 seconds a mile slower for every 5 degrees above 60°F or for every 2 degrees above 15°C).

Question

What should be the long run schedule for a "to finish" (or first) marathon?

Answer

Count back from the date of the marathon, using this schedule. This assumes that the runner is starting with a longest run in the past two weeks of 3 miles.

1. 3 miles
2. 4,5 miles
3. 3 miles
4. 6 miles
5. 3 miles
6. 7,5 miles
7. 3 miles
8. 9 miles
9. 4 miles
10. 10,5 miles
11. 4 miles
12. 12 miles
13. 4 miles
14. 13,5 miles
15. 5 miles
16. 15 miles
17. 5 miles with a MM (magic mile time trial)*
18. 17 miles
19. 6 miles
20. 7 miles with a MM
21. 20 miles
22. 6 miles
23. 7 miles with a MM
24. 23 miles
25. 6 miles
26. 7 miles with a MM
27. 26 miles
28. 6 miles
29. 7 miles
30. Goal Marathon Weekend

*Note:

The "magic mile" is explained in the answer to the question about estimating current performance. For more schedule and training information, see my book RUNNING – A YEAR ROUND PLAN.

Question

How many weeks are needed for a marathon training program?

Answer

It is best to work from the distance of your longest long run in the last 2 weeks. Mark where this distance matches the long run list on the schedule in the answer to the last question. You may start on the next week. So a runner who has recently run 10 miles could start the program at week # 11 or week # 12.

Question

Should first-time marathoners try for a time goal?

Answer

I don't recommend this. The finishing of the marathon is one of life's great experiences. When you try to run a challenging time, you will reduce the overall reward effect of this experience.

Question
Should first time marathoners do speedwork during the training period?

Answer
No. Speedwork dramatically increases the chance of injury, and is not needed to finish a marathon.

Question
Must I rest completely the day before long runs?

Answer
As the long runs get longer it becomes more important to rest the day before.

SECTION 7:
RUNNING
A FASTER
MARATHON

Question

How much can I expect to improve during a 6 month training program?

Answer

Most of the time goal runners I've worked with over the past 35 years have improved between 3% and 5% during a 6 month program when they have done the long runs and speed sessions as noted in my book RUNNING – A YEAR ROUND PLAN. So if everything goes well in training and on race day, a 15 to 30 second per mile improvement is possible. Weather and crowds can cause a slowdown in the finish time. (60°F/15°C or below is ideal). I usually allow my e-coach clients to set a maximum goal of a 30 second improvement, if they wish. But if the magic mile is not showing this type of improvement as the goal approaches, I suggest attempting a goal no faster than predicted.

Question

How many days per week do I need in a time improvement program?

Answer

I've found that time goal runners only need 3 running days per week. If you want to run 4 or 5 days a week this is usually OK as long as recovery is proceeding well and there are no aches and pains. There should be a day of rest before the long runs, and the speed sessions.

Question

What is the longest distance of a long run, which will help me improve my time?

Answer

To maximize endurance and performance, I suggest building the long one up to 29 miles. In surveys, I've found that there's an average of 11 minutes of time improvement when a runner increases the length of the last long training run from 26 miles to 29 miles. The pace of these long runs should be at least 2 min/mile slower than current marathon finish time – with the run-walk-run strategy appropriate to the pace. The last long run should be done 3-4 weeks before the marathon.

Question
What type of speed training will help?

Answer

The type of speedwork that has helped my runners the most is a form of interval training called "mile repetitions." The training format is detailed in RUNNING – A YEAR ROUND PLAN, and GALLOWAY TRAINING PROGRAMS. Once the muscles are warmed up, each timed mile is run 30 seconds faster than goal pace, followed by a 5 minute rest interval of walking and/or jogging. Starting with 4-mile repetitions, the number is increased during each successive workout to a maximum of 14. These workouts are done on non-long-run weekends – in most cases the weekend after the long run.

Question
Should I take walk breaks during the mile repetions?

Answer

Walk breaks are inserted into each mile repetition as follows: run the amount planned during the race itself, but walk half of the amount. For example, a runner training for a 10:30 pace in the marathon would be running 10:00 for each mile repeat, using a run-walk-run strategy of (run 3 minutes/walk 30 seconds). In the race this runner should be running for 3 minutes/walking for 1 minute. I don't recommend that first time marathoners attempt a time goal or do mile repetitions.

Question

Are there any drills that can help me run faster, by improving my running form?

Answer

As noted in my books RUNNING – A YEAR ROUND PLAN, HALF MARATHON, 5K/10K, I've discovered two drills that can help runners improve their running form: "cadence drill (CD)" and "acceleration-gliders (Acg)." Both are done 4-8 times, at least once a week, on a short mileage day.

The CD: Time yourself for 30 seconds. During this period, count how many times your left or right foot touches the ground (pick one before you start). On each successive thirty-second segment, try to increase the count by 1 or 2.

The Acg: Jog slowly for 10 steps, jog a little faster for 10 steps, then gradually increase speed to your magic mile pace for 10-15 steps and let your momentum carry you as you gradually slow down to a jog again (the glide).

A 30-60 second jog or walk can be done between each. No sprinting. The goal in the CD is simply to increase the count by being more efficient. The Acg goal is to learn how to use momentum to conserve resources.

Question

How should I schedule my long runs and mile repeats to run faster in the marathon?

Answer

All of the key workouts are done on the weekends. Long runs alternate with mile repeats, and the "magic mile" is scheduled on the third weekend. Here is how it works for a runner whose long run at the beginning of the training program is 5 miles.

Time Goal Schedule of weekend workouts

1. 6 miles
2. 3 miles
3. 7,5 mile
4. 4 miles
5. 9 miles
6. 4 miles
7. 10,5 miles
8. 5 miles
9. 12 miles
10. 5 miles
11. 13,5 miles
12. 5 miles
13. 15 miles
14. 4 x 1 mile
15. 17 miles
16. 6 x 1 mile
17. 7 miles with a MM (magic mile time trial)*
18. 20 miles
19. 8 x 1 mile
20. 7 miles with a MM
21. 23 miles
22. 10 x 1 mile
23. 7 miles with a MM
24. 26 miles
25. 12 x 1 mile
26. 7 miles with a MM
27. 29 miles
28. 6 miles
29. 14 x 1 mile
30. 7 miles
31. Goal Marathon Weekend

*Note:

The "magic mile" is explained in the answer to the question about estimating current performance.

Question
If my long run is longer than 6 miles, can I start closer to the end of the program?

Answer

Yes. For example, if you have run 12 miles within the last 2 weeks, you could start at week # 10 or week # 11.

Question
Do any of the cross-training exercises help one run faster?

Answer

Water running can help runners improve running form. The resistance of the water forces the legs to find a more efficient path. Put on a flotation device and go to the deep end of a swimming pool (usually at least 5.5 feet deep). Move your legs in a running motion that replicates how you run on land – no knee lift, extending your leg a little forward, feet low but kick out a little in front, and bring the whole leg behind as the lower leg moves behind you. Start with 5-10 minutes and build up to 15-30 minutes. You can do this workout on a non-running day, or as a second workout on a running day.

Question
When do I practice running at race pace?

Answer

I recommend that time goal runners insert one or two "race rehearsal" segments during one or two of the short runs each week (usually on Tuesday and Thursday). Pick a measured course so that you can time yourself at goal pace, taking the walk breaks as you will do them in the marathon itself.

Question
Would it be helpful to run a really hard half marathon (or similar distance) before my marathon goal race?

Answer

Unfortunately, the lingering fatigue from a hard effort in a race longer than 8K can compromise the quality and recovery from the various training components. It is best to stay with the plan in my books (see list at www.JeffGalloway.com). I've found that the mile repeat workouts do a better job of preparing for a faster marathon as opposed to running a long race, such as the half marathon.

SECTION 8:
THE RACE ITSELF:
- CHOOSING YOUR RACE
- THE DAY BEFORE THE RACE
- RACE DAY

Question

How should I choose a marathon if I want to run a fast time?

Answer

Avoid crowded races. Most runners in the large population events run more than three-quarters of a mile farther than marathon distance. Since you don't get credit for the extra distance, it is harder to run goal pace in these venues. Look for smaller marathons that have a good record for producing fast times. Visit

www.marathonguide.com

and

www.RunnersWorld.com

for a lot of information with runner reviews, which are usually quite revealing. Courses that have slight upgrades of short duration allow for a varied use of muscle groups, which often helps in reducing muscle fatigue. There are many downhill courses that can help speed you up – if you train on downhill courses. While you cannot control the weather, look for venues that tend to have high temperatures of 60°F (15°C) or cooler during the month when you are running your race.

Question
How do the crowds in a race slow you down?

Answer

Courses are measured on the straightest line, cutting the tangents from turn to turn. Every time you deviate from this very direct route between two points, you add distance. In crowded marathons runners have to move around constantly, weaving in and out of other runners. Many of my e-coach clients have worn GPS and accelerometer technology devices. The amount of extra distance covered is between .75 and 1 mile farther for most. Large races are fun, give you a great tour of most cities, and are supported by crowds that make the experience motivating and interesting. But small races are better venues for running fast.

Question
Where can I find information on races with runner reviews?

Answer

The websites most commonly used by my runners are

www.marathonguide.com

and

www.RunnersWorld.com

There is a lot of information about most races in each of these. Be sure to read the runner reviews. It also helps to visit a technical running store. Staff members hear stories and details about races that often don't get reported in other places-such as "how long it takes to get to the start on race day" and "they didn't have enough porto-johns." Veteran runners, who have attended many races, can often give editorial advice and steer you toward other information resources.

Question

What other factors are important in choosing a race?

Answer

There are several factors you cannot control, which can slow your running pace – especially weather and terrain. Visit one of the sites, such as www.marathonguide.com for course profiles showing ups and downs. While you cannot predict the weather, research the area for the average high temperature, and other weather trends for that time of year. This will help you prepare for race day as you pack your bag. There are a series of items that can help you choose, and plan, in my book RUNNING – A YEAR ROUND PLAN.

Question
How far ahead of the race do I need to enter?

Answer

As soon as you decide to enter a race, enroll yourself. A growing number of races are limiting the field – and this is a good thing for runners if they enter early. The larger the enrollment, the more challenging the logistics. On some of the race websites you can find information about how many entries are left, and when the race closed its enrollment in previous years.

Question
How do I enter a race?

Answer

Go to the race website and follow the directions. Most races allow you to enter online, for a small fee. There is often the option of printing an entry form and sending it in. If you live near the race organizer, you may be able to register in person, at race headquarters or at a sponsor's outlet. Again, look at the race website.

The Day Before The Race

Question
What should I eat?

Answer

Practice your eating plan the day before the long runs. After 5 or 6 pre-race eating days, you should have a plan that works for you. Avoid eating a lot of food after about 2pm the day before. If you get hungry, eat a snack that can be digested easily, about every 2-3 hours. Since it takes about 36-48 hours for food to be digested, metabolized, etc., the food you eat the day before will not help you during the race – and too much of it can hurt you.

Question
What is the worst eating problem the day before?

Answer

Eating too much food during the afternoon or evening before the race can reduce your performance and require extra potty stops. When you eat a lot of food the day before, most of it will be in the gut the next morning. This will require some blood flow for digestion, diverting blood that could be bringing oxygen to the exercising muscles. In addition, some embarrassing things can happen when your gut is loaded up and you are bouncing up and down for several hours. Practice eating the day before long runs using small meals or snacks of food that can be easily digested. Avoid fatty food, high fiber items, too much dairy, and any foods that have caused you problems before.

Question

What should I drink the day before the long run or race, and when?

Answer

The day before a long run/race you want to keep fluid flowing through your body. I recommend drinking 6-8 oz (200 ml) of water or sports drinks, every 1-2 hours. It's a good idea to have at least 16 oz of sports drink throughout the day before the long run. Accelerade has been shown to maintain hydration levels, compared to a leading sports drink and water.

Question

How much running/walking should I do the day before long runs and the marathon itself?

Answer

You don't need to run or walk at all the day before the race. You're not going to improve your conditioning during this period. But most runners I've heard from on this issue find that gentle walking, for 1-2 miles, promotes circulation in the legs. This is the amount that most runners walk when they attend a race expo. Practice some gentle walking the day before your long runs and go with what works best.

Question
What if I don't sleep the night before?

Answer

I've heard from countless runners who cannot sleep the night before the marathon. A few have felt that this may have hurt their performance, but this is usually due to negative thinking, in my opinion. Most of the reports of pre-race insomnia include a strong race performance the next day. Many have set personal records. When one has had several nights without sleep, in a row, there might be a fatigue problem. Otherwise, don't worry about it. Bring a book, watch a DVD, or play a game.

Question
Should I bring a dry pair of socks on a rainy day?

Answer

When socks and shoes get soaked, the misery index increases dramatically. It helps to have, in your fanny pack, a spare pair of socks, in a baggie. For a real treat, have someone meet you on the course at 13-20 miles with a dry pair of shoes.

Question
How should I pace myself?

Answer

If this is your first marathon, I recommend running at a conservative training pace-adding two minutes to the pace predicted by the magic mile (as an all-out pace), and adjust for temperatures above 60°F (15°C) (see the answer to the next question). If you're attempting a time goal, and have done all of the training elements correctly, take your best magic mile time during the last month of training, multiply by 1.3 and adjust for non-ideal conditions such as crowds, hills and temperature (as noted in the next answer). It is always best to run 10-20 seconds per mile slower than you believe you can run, during the first 5-6 miles.

Question
What is a "negative split"?

Answer

When you run the second half a race faster than the first half, you have run a "negative split." This means that the second half is faster than the first half. This strong finish results from backing off the pace enough during the first half, usually by 10-20 seconds per mile.

Question

Why does a "negative split" produce faster times?

Answer

By running a bit slower than you could currently run in the marathon from the beginning, you will save resources (muscle fuel, feet, joints, muscles, tendons). Whatever you save in the first half will be available for use during the second half. Most runners I've surveyed, who have run more than 5 marathons, ran their fastest marathon by using this strategy. So, a smart pacer will run about 20 seconds per mile slower than goal pace during the first 4-6 miles. If everything is going well at that point, increase the per-mile pace to 5-10 seconds slower than goal pace for another 5 miles. At that point, increase to the pace you believe you can average for the rest of the marathon. After mile # 18, you can run as you wish. Whatever you have saved in the first half you can spend during the last 6-8 miles on race day.

Question
How should I adjust pace for warm temperatures?

Answer

Over the years I've tabulated the slowdown due to heat increase. The rule of thumb is to slow down 30 seconds a mile for every 5 degrees above 60°F (15°C). Many runners bring thermometers or hand-held devices that can access temperature, so that they can make these adjustments. It is crucial to slow down starting at 65°F (18°C) to avoid a greater slowdown at the end of the race.

Question
Should the walk breaks be adjusted as the pace slows down?

Answer

Yes. As the pace becomes slower, the walk breaks should be taken more frequently. I suggest using the following ratio of running and walking, according to the pace per mile:

7 min/mi-run 1 mile, walk 30-45 seconds
7:30/mi-run 5 minutes, walk 30-45 seconds
8:00/mi-run 4 minutes, walk 30 seconds
8:30/mi-run 4 minutes, walk 45 seconds
9:00/mi-run 4 minutes, walk 1 minute (4-1)
10:00/mi-run 3 minutes, walk 1 minute
11:00/mi-2:30-1
12:00/mi-2-1
13:00/mi-1-1
14:00/mi-30 seconds-30 seconds
15:00/mi-30 seconds run-45 seconds walk
16:00/mi-20 sec run-40 sec walk
17:00/mi-15 sec run-45 sec walk
18:00/mi-10 sec run-50 sec walk

Note:

It is always OK to take more frequent walk breaks than listed.

Question
How does cold weather affect pacing?

Answer

When the temperature is below 60°F (15°C), the body can release the heat generated by running. This allows you to run faster with less discomfort. By using the correct number of layers, most runners can feel warm enough – even during very cold weather. As the temperature drops below 40°F (4°C) some runners feel a "misery index" due to chill. In most cases, wearing adjustable layers, such as a long sleeve outer garment, allows you to cool off by removing layers. The long sleeve T-shirt can be removed when you warm up, tied around the waist-available for use if you are cool later. By using clothing to stay comfortable, one can adjust and expand your acceptable temperature range.

Caution:

Wearing too many layers or not peeling them off soon enough can result in heat stress, slowing down and risk of heat disease. Be sure to remove a layer at the first sign that your body temperature is rising.

Question
What should I eat during the race?

Answer

Unfortunately, very little of the food and fluid you consume during a run can be used during that run. Running a marathon puts enough stress on the system to shut down the digestive tract. It is possible to absorb a small amount of fluid, and blood sugar booster, every 15 minutes or so, and this can help you stay motivated. Your brain needs glycogen as fuel. Long runs will significantly reduce the available supply of this limited resource. But by consuming blood sugar boosting foods (gel products, hard candies, gummy bears, energy bars) you can maintain mental focus and avoid some of the negative messages at the end of your race. Practice taking several products during long runs to find what works best for you. This allows each runner to discover the best source, the amount, the quantity of water, the frequency and how to adjust as the distance increases. A rule of thumb, based upon the runners I've worked with, is the following: 30-40 calories every 1-2 miles, starting with mile 5.

Question
What if I have nausea when I eat anything before running?

Answer

1. Don't eat anything before a run.

2. Drink water only, before and during runs, and limit the amount to 10-18 oz an hour.

3. Eat smaller amounts of your blood sugar booster more frequently than you have been doing.

Question
What should I drink during the race, and how much?

Answer

It is important to drink regularly – at least every 15 minutes – but don't drink too much. The maximum recommended by marathon medical directors is no more than 27 oz an hour – but the runners that I've worked with average about half this much. Water is absorbed quicker than other fluids. Water also results in a lower risk of nausea.

Question
Should I bring my own water during the marathon?

Answer

You will always have more control over your destiny by carrying a water bottle that can be refilled at water stops. This allows you to drink when you want to drink. Practice several different types of bottles, or water carrying products, on your training runs to see what works best for you.

Question
Should I take salt tablets?

Answer

Those who experience muscle cramps at the end of runs, or have experienced hyponatremia should consider taking salt tablets. Most of my e-coach clients who suffered from muscle cramps found that a slower starting pace and more frequent walk breaks allowed them to avoid this problem. But when the cramping continued, salt tablets have helped. The best product, according to my experience, is a buffered tablet called Succeed, which contains both sodium and potassium.

Question
Coffee:
Do I have to give up caffeine?

Answer

Caffeine has been shown to enhance performance and endurance among distance runners (1-2 cups, 1-2 hours before the start). Those who have problems with caffeine should avoid it. But if you like your cup of coffee before a run, continue to enjoy it. You'll need to find the right consumption timetable so that you can avoid unnecessary potty stops. In other words, stop drinking the coffee early enough so that you can go to the rest room before the start of your run.

Question
Alcohol:
Do I have to give up alcohol?

Answer

Alcohol is a central nervous system depressant which leaves one dehydrated. It's not recommended to consume beer, wine, etc., the afternoon or evening before a long run, or within 2 hours after a workout or race that has resulted in significant dehydration. Otherwise, a glass of wine or a beer at night is an individual choice. Moderation is the key.

Question
What should I wear?

Answer

In my books, especially RUNNING – A YEAR ROUND PLAN & RUNNING UNTIL YOU'RE 100, you will find a "clothing thermometer." This has been a great guide for adjusting clothing to temperature.

Question
What should I wear while waiting for the start of a race if it is raining or cold?

Answer

It helps to bring a garbage bag with you to the start of the marathon. In case of rain or cold weather, make a hole for the head and use the bag to stay dry and warm. Put on enough layers so that you can stay warm before the start.

Question
What should I wear during a run, when it is raining?

Answer

Next to your skin, wear a garment that can move the moisture away from the body. There are many technical fibers, such as Mizuno's "breath thermo" which will release most of the moisture received from precipitation and will warm up as it gets wet. Be sure to remove the garbage bag and other extra layers when you start running. Be sure to discard it at the side of the road so that other runners will not have problems with this on the road.

Question
What about wet feet/shoes during a rainy race?

Answer

If you can have someone meet you between 13 and 18 miles with a dry pair of shoes, this is wonderful. There is some relief from replacing wet socks with a dry pair that you can carry in your fanny pack.

Question
How do I choose the best shoe for me?

Answer

The best advice is... to get the best advice. Running shoe designers use a complicated mix of orthopedic features to support and protect specific types of feet while running. The best running stores continuously train employees on how to match up feet with specific shoes based upon function and fit. Over the past 35+ years, my staff members at Phidippides, in Atlanta GA, have found that a trained observer can solve fitting problems, and offer adjustments for the unique motions of the individual foot. Take the information from your shoe advisor and choose the shoe that works best on your feet.

Question
When do I replace a shoe?

Answer

As soon as you are satisfied with your current running shoe, run back to the store and get an identical pair. Because the shoe companies change their models about every 9 months, an experienced running store person can help you find a model with the same characteristics as before. Each week, during the last mile of one of your short workouts, run in the new pair. This will gradually allow the new pair to "break in." After several weeks you will know that your old shoe is losing support, because you have the direct comparison in the running motion. Be sure to shift to the newer pair before the old one is totally worn out. Then, start breaking in the next pair.

SECTION 10: STRENGTHENING, STRETCHING & CROSS-TRAINING

Note: Stretching can cause injury

Question Do I need to add strength training?

Answer

I've not found it necessary to do strength work during a marathon training program. Based upon my experience and research, endurance running is based upon the efficient use of momentum, and the long runs produce the minimal strength necessary for the marathon challenge. For long-term health, I suggest postural muscle strengthening. I use the exercises noted in the next four answers.

Question

I don't feel strong in the last portion of a long run – what strength exercises will give me strength at this point?

Answer

I've not found that strength exercises will help you in this situation. To be strong during the last 6 miles:

1. Increase the distance of your last long run to 29 miles, as noted in RUNNING – A YEAR ROUND PLAN.

2. Pace yourself more conservatively during the first 10 miles of the marathon.

3. Insert walk breaks more frequently from the beginning of the marathon.

Question

What is the best exercise to strengthen the stomach muscles?

Answer

The exercise called "the crunch" can build strength throughout the front side of the body, down to the hips and pelvic area. The "crunch" is done while lying on the floor, on one's back. Bend the knees and bring the head and shoulders slightly off the floor, and ease back down. It's best to keep going up and down in a very short range of motion so that the stomach muscles are continuously being used to move the weight of the body up or down.

Question

How can I strengthen the shoulders, neck and backmuscles?

The exercise I call "arm running" can reduce shoulder fatigue on long runs and help one maintain upright body posture. It strengthens the muscles on the backside of your upper body with connections to the spine. While holding hand-held weights, in the standing position, move your arms through a natural running motion. You should not feel any pressure or exertion in any specific muscle group. Pick an amount of weight that leaves you feeling that you got a workout but doesn't cause you to strain to do a set of 10 (one count means that the left and the right hand have gone through the cycle).

Question
What stretches should I do?

Answer

Surprisingly, I've found that stretching causes many injuries. I don't believe that most runners or walkers benefit from stretching. So I'm going to take away the guilt for not stretching. If you have some stretches that help you and don't produce aches and pains, then do them – but be careful.

Question
What about yoga or pilates?

Answer

I hear from many runners every year who are injured in yoga or pilates classes. I don't see any benefit for most runners in these activities. But if you do them (and are not experiencing problems), be careful.

Question
Is it necessary to do cross-training?

Answer

Most of the runners I've worked with did not need to do any cross-training. The long runs build endurance, and the short runs serve to maintain the adaptations. Cross-training will improve overall health and fitness, but this does not have any effect on marathon improvement if my training schedule is used.

Question
Are there any cross-training exercises to avoid?

Answer

On the non-running days, it's best to avoid exercises that use the calf muscles: stair machines, step aerobics and spinning. Maximum recovery of the calf muscle occurs when the muscle is not used in a workout for 48 hours.

Question
Are there any cross-training exercises that improve running?

Answer

Water running can help you improve your running form. As you move your legs through the running motion, the resistance of the water forces the legs and feet to find a more efficient path.

Question
How do I run in the water?

Answer

Get a floatation device and move to a part of the pool where your feet don't touch the bottom. Move your legs through a range of motion that is similar to an efficient distance running stride: kick the legs a bit out in front, bring each leg behind, but don't lift your knees. The resistance of the water will force your legs to find a more efficient path as you move your legs. Monitor your breathing rate as a measure of exertion. You want to breathe at about the same rate as when running one of your short runs as on Tuesday or Thursday.

SECTION 11: MOTIVATION

Question

How can I deal with the negative messages before a run?

Answer

Your "left brain" is composed of logical and stress monitoring segments in the brain. Its job is to steer you into pleasure and away from discomfort. As the discomfort level rises during a run, this side of the brain starts pinging you with a stream of messages to "slow down," "stop," etc. Before long runs and other challenging workouts it helps to rehearse these, which will desensitize you to them before or during the race itself. As you overcome each challenge you will develop more confidence the next time. Talk back to the left brain and you will gain more control over your confidence: "Be quiet, left brain, I know that you are going to bother me. I will be successful." Mentally rehearse the morning of the marathon, many times. Go through the preparation ritual that has worked on your long runs, rehearsing the left-brain nagging messages, and your positive responses. Come out of each rehearsal with the image of yourself running away from the starting line, feeling good, looking forward to the run.

Question

How can I keep going when motivation is low during a run?

Answer

There will be periods of low confidence during some training runs, and the marathon itself – even when the training has fully prepared you for the event. Here is a plan that can be practiced in advance, that has helped runners push through to the finish:

1. Don't give up! Confront doubt by keeping the feet moving and saying "I can do it."

2. If your training has not been as good as it should have been, back off the pace early and take more frequent walk breaks than usual – to save resources for the end.

3. When the going gets tough, don't focus on how much farther-just the next running segment ("Three more minutes").

4. If the amount of the running segment is still tough, keep reducing the amount until you know you can do it ("One more minute" or "Thirty more seconds").

5. There have been some race situations when I've had to go down to "One more step" to get through a rough patch. This got me through.

6. Don't push through a real medical issue, as you could make the situation much worse.

Question

What can you say to yourself to help during the tough parts of a marathon?

Answer

Most of us have had recurring problems during long runs or races. When we mentally connect a few magic words to our successful experiences we are empowered by a boost of confidence. I use the words "relax, power and glide" to confront three recurring problems I've had over the past 40 years:

1. When I struggle too hard to maintain pace on a tough day, my muscles tighten up.

2. Fatigue causes a slowdown and I lose confidence that I can finish as I had planned.

3. My form gets ragged at the end of a difficult run.

Each time I've been successful in overcoming one of these problems I've associated the three words with the successful experience. When I say the three words now, my brain is flooded with positive memories and feelings of confidence, which often carry me for a mile or two. You can pull out successes from your memory bank or use the victories of others. The more experiences, the longer you will feel the effect of these words. See my books TESTING YOURSELF, GALLOWAY'S BOOK ON RUNNING & GALLOWAY TRAINING PROGRAM for more information on "magic words."

Question
Are there some mental tricks to get through the last few miles?

Answer

I call these "dirty tricks." When you are under stress, you will receive an increasing number of messages from the left brain, telling you to slow down, quit or abandon your goal. These tricks act as quick fixes that distract the left brain, reducing the effect of the distracting and unmotivating messages. It helps to think ahead and have a few of these in place during any run that could be challenging.

My most popular dirty trick is the "giant invisible rubber band." When someone passes me, and the left brain starts telling me that "I don't have it," I lasso them with this instrument that I have in my fanny pack or wrapped around my waist. I visualize looping the person around the neck, which should slow them down. As I pull on the imagined rubber band, I straighten up and breathe better while focusing on the person ahead. At some point in this process, the left brain breaks through, telling me that my rubber band trick is not a logical concept, and I have to laugh at myself. But laughing activates the creative right brain, opening up solutions and sources of strength. Also important is the fact that I am getting closer and closer to the finish.

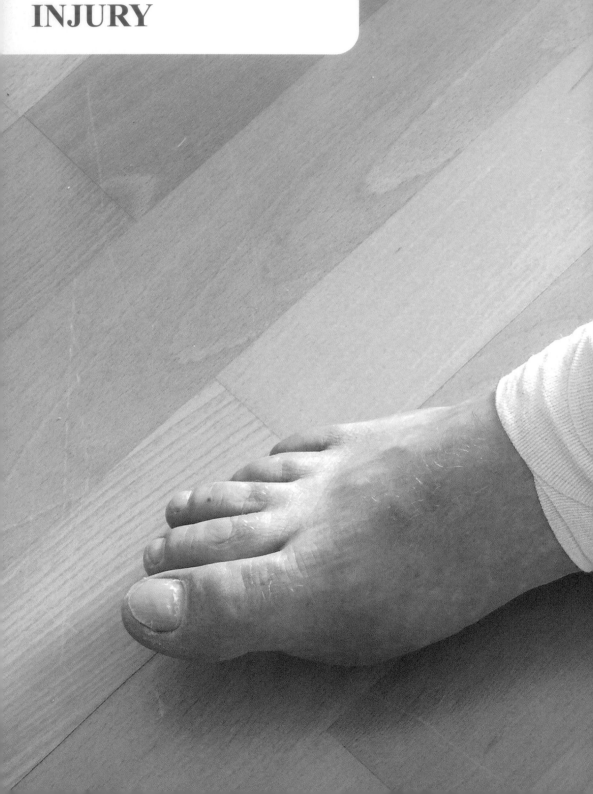

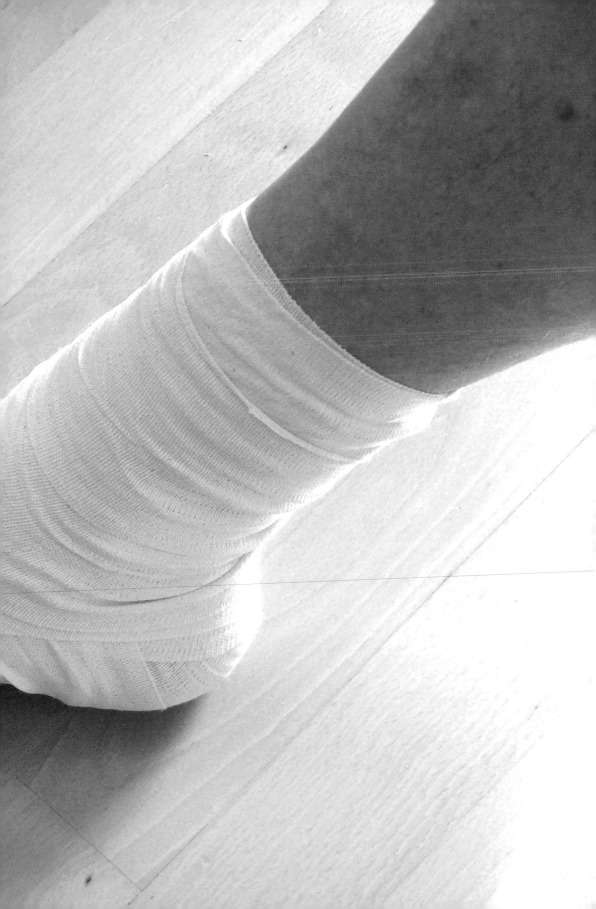

Note:

The following advice is given as one runner to another. For medical advice, see a doctor.

Question
What are the reasons why marathoners get injured?

Answer

1. Running the long runs too fast. (See the question on pacing the long runs). Running at least two min/mi slower than current marathon race pace is usually slow enough to reduce injury risk. But it is safer to run even slower than this.

2. Not inserting walk breaks frequently enough. When runners go from a run 5 minutes/walk 1 minute strategy to a 3-1, they reduce injury risk by about 50%. Dropping to 1-1 drops the risk to almost nothing.

3. Speed training increases injury risk.

4. Stretching increases the chance of injury. Unless you have found stretches that you know are necessary for you (and don't cause aches and pains), I don't recommend stretching.

5. For more information see A WOMAN'S GUIDE TO RUNNING, RUNNING UNTIL YOU'RE 100, and GALLOWAY'S BOOK ON RUNNING.

Question
How do you tell whether it is an injury?

Answer

There are three signs that you probably have an injury. I recommend taking at least 3 days off from running if you notice any of the following:

1. Inflammation-swelling in an area that is used when running.

2. Loss of function – the knee, foot, etc. doesn't work the way it should.

3. Pain during a run, or afterward, that does not go away or gets worse as you run.

Question

How much time should I take off from running if I suspect an injury?

Answer

If you are concerned that this could be an injury, take 5 days off from running. If you feel that there is a small amount of damage, take 3 days off. With effective treatment during this time off, you can usually get the healing started. If you stay below the threshold of further irritation, most runners can run while the injury is healing.

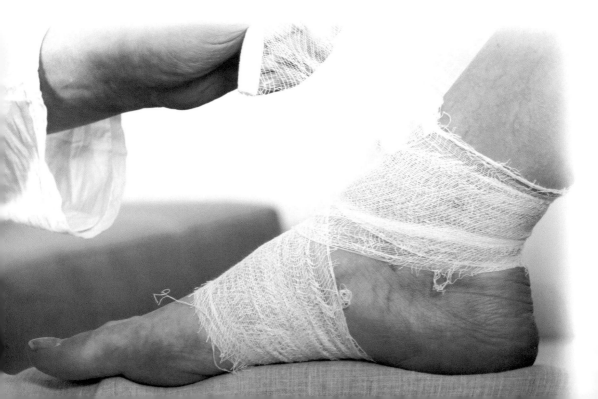

Question
What should one do when injured?

Answer

1. Take at least 3 days of no running to get the healing started.

2. See a doctor who is knowledgeable about the type of injury you have. The sooner you can get an accurate diagnosis, the sooner you can treat it in an appropriate way.

3. In most cases, my runners have been able to continue running while an injury heals, by inserting a lot more walking into the run-walk-run ratio – and running a lot slower.

4. To allow for healing, you must stay below the threshold of further irritation.

5. Run no more often than every other day.

6. Avoid any activity that could irritate the injured area.

Question How should I treat knee pain?

Answer

Because there are many different types of knee problems, it's best to get a good diagnosis. If the pain is inside the knee, ask the doctor if anti-inflammatory medication could help. If your feet roll inward as you push off, you may benefit from some type of orthotic.

An injury on the outside of the knee diagnosed as Iliotibial Band syndrome can be helped by using a foam roller (there's a picture on www.JeffGalloway.com showing how to use this). If the knee tightens up during a run, there are some stretches that can help (illustrated in GETTING STARTED).

There is a more thorough discussion of knee issues in GALLOWAY'S BOOK ON RUNNING 2ND ED

Question
How should I treat shin pain?

Answer

Worst case is when the pain is the result of a stress fracture. Generally, this means that the pain increases as you run farther. If you suspect that you may have a stress fracture, see a doctor.

Most shin pain is due to overuse of the anterior or posterior tibial muscles on the front or the inside of the lower leg. There is usually no long term damage in this case, just pain. Most of my runners have been able to run through shin injuries when they trained below the threshold of further irritation – slowing down, taking walk breaks much more frequently and making form adjustments (shorten stride, keep feet low to the ground, run with more of a "shuffle.") It is best not to do any racing or speed training if you want the shin pain to disappear.

Front of shin: This is often due to having a stride that is too long for your level of conditioning-whether walking or running. The most common running segment when the stride is too long is during the last 25% of a run, and on downhill runs. Shorten stride to baby steps, and keep your feet low to the ground.

Question
How do I treat heel pain?

Answer

The most common heel pain is due to "plantar fasciitis." Those suffering from this problem usually feel pain on the inside or middle of the heel early in the morning. If you experience this, put on a supportive shoe before stepping out of bed each morning and don't walk barefooted. I've found that stretching tends to keep the foot injured and prolongs the healing process in most of the runners that I've advised.

Pain on the back or side of the heel can be due to an irritation of the Achilles tendon. See the next question for a discussion of this injury. The ice massage – right on the spot that hurts – has been the most effective treatment.

The "toe squincher" exercise can help to prevent plantar injury in the future. This exercise is performed by pointing your foot and contracting the muscles in your foot (15-20 times throughout the day). Doing this for a few seconds will usually result in cramping of these muscles. As they become stronger and stronger, they provide more support, taking pressure off the plantar and other stabilizing components.

Question
What should I do if the Achilles tendon hurts?

Answer

This tendon wraps under and around the back of the heel bone, forming a thick band that connects to the calf muscle. If you don't stretch it, and rub a chunk of ice directly on it for 15 minutes every night (whether you run or not), healing can usually proceed. Note: Ice bags and gel ice don't tend to bestow any benefit. For the best healing effect, rub the ice cube directly on the Achilles, constantly rubbing for 15 minutes. If the tendon is significantly injured, you may need to stop running and all activities that significantly use the Achilles tendon (including walking up stairs) for 5-7 days.

Question
What if I have sore (or painful) hamstrings?

Answer

This muscle and tendon band behind the thigh is often aggravated when we stretch, or run fast. Don't do any activity that could stretch it. Massage can often speed up the healing – even using a massage instrument like "the stick." Run with a short stride, touching lightly with your feet. Be sure to insert more frequent walk breaks.

Question What if I have a sore back or neck?

Answer

In many cases, these two areas are irritated by a forward lean. Try to run "like a puppet on a string." As you come out of a walk break, take a breath and imagine that you are being suspended from above the top of your head so that the hips, shoulders and head are in alignment.

Running with a stride that is too long for you can also cause back and neck pain due to a twisting motion of the hips.

If you suffer from chronic pain in these areas, I recommend reading the book THE MIND-BODY PRESCRIPTION by Dr. John Sarno.

Question
What should I do about sore feet?

Answer

Try inserting a more protective foot support system in your shoe. The Spenco insole, for example, has been effective in foot protection. If the problem persists, see a very experienced podiatrist who has treated a lot of runners, because there are many different problems that could occur in your feet. The good news is that there are many simple solutions, or coping mechanisms, that can allow you to run without making a condition worse. See my books RUNNING UNTIL YOU'RE 100 & GALLOWAY'S BOOK ON RUNNING 2ND ED for more information.

1. Inspect the skin. Certain areas that are thicker than others can be a cause of pain. Removing the callous with a pumice stone or similar instrument can be a simple fix for this.

2. Metatarsal pain is usually found in the widest part of the forefoot, where the toe joints line up. An ice massage every night, for 15 minutes can often help. Rub in circles, on the area that hurts.

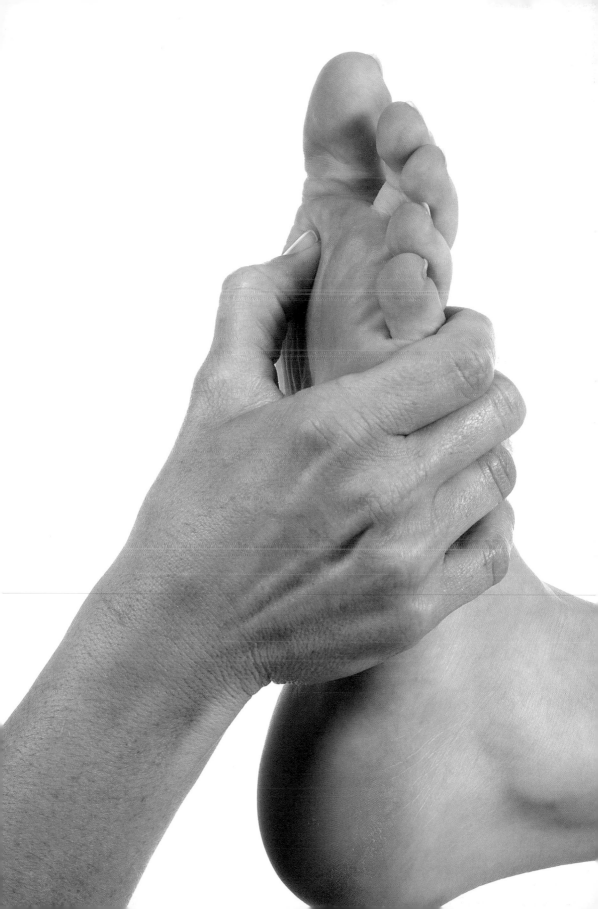

SECTION 13:
RUNNING FORM

Question
Is there a way to run that reduces aches and pains?

Answer

If you are not having problems, you should run the way that works for you. The suggestions below are only directed at those who have aches, pains or other posture-related problems. Your body usually finds the best pattern of running, intuitively, if you don't push it out of its normal range of motion.

Question
What is the best running posture?

Answer

Upright posture tends to be best: head over shoulders, over hips, as the feet touch lightly underneath. A forward lean often results in back or neck pain, and can force one to shorten stride length.

Question
How much can I bounce off the ground?

Answer

The most efficient stride is more of a shuffle, in which the feet stay right next to the ground.

Question
Should I run on my heels or on my forefoot?

Answer

Each of us has a natural pattern of running that is unique to the individual. It's best to let the feet move naturally. When runners who naturally land on the heel try to run only on the forefoot, there are often injuries.

Question
If I naturally pronate, should I get a motion control shoe or orthotic?

Answer

Those who don't have aches and pains, even when they severely overpronate, have probably adjusted to this motion. Only when you have pain that is the result of overpronation would I recommend getting a motion control or stability shoe. Be sure to go to a running store that has the most knowledgeable staff in your area.

Extreme problems relating to pronation should be attended to by a knowledgeable podiatrist. Most of the top podiatrists I have worked with don't put runners in an orthotic right away. They try several moderate control adjustments before casting a hard device.

Question
What is the most efficient stride for reducing effort and running faster?

Answer

The range of motion of your legs should be minimal, with feet low to the ground and a light touch of the feet. This tends to reduce effort, while it helps you avoid aches and pains. The foot should absorb your body weight directly underneath you, as the back leg swings behind. Your foot should not rise above a 90 degree angle made by the body and the lower leg, when behind. There should be no knee lift, and almost no use of the quadracep muscle.

Question
Is there a drill that can help improve your leg turnover, or cadence?

Answer

The "cadence drill" will help you improve running efficiency, as you increase the number of steps per minute.

- ■ Warm up for 10 min of easy running.

- ■ While running, time yourself for 30 seconds, counting how many times your left or right foot touches the ground.

- ■ Walk for 30-60 seconds between each.

- ■ Try to increase the count by 1 or 2 on each successive 30-second count.

- ■ Do 4-8 of these, one day a week, every week.

Question

Is there an exercise that can help you conserve energy when running faster?

Answer

Yes, I call this drill the Acceleration-Glider:

- Warm up with 10 minutes of easy running.

- Start each acceleration with approximately 10 steps of slow running.

- Then, increase the pace slightly for approximately 10 steps.

- Next, for about 15 steps or so, increase to a 5K race pace (no sprinting).

- Then coast off your momentum, gradually slowing down over the next 20 or 30 steps.

- This helps to develop muscles and mechanisms for faster running, as you learn how to save energy by gliding.

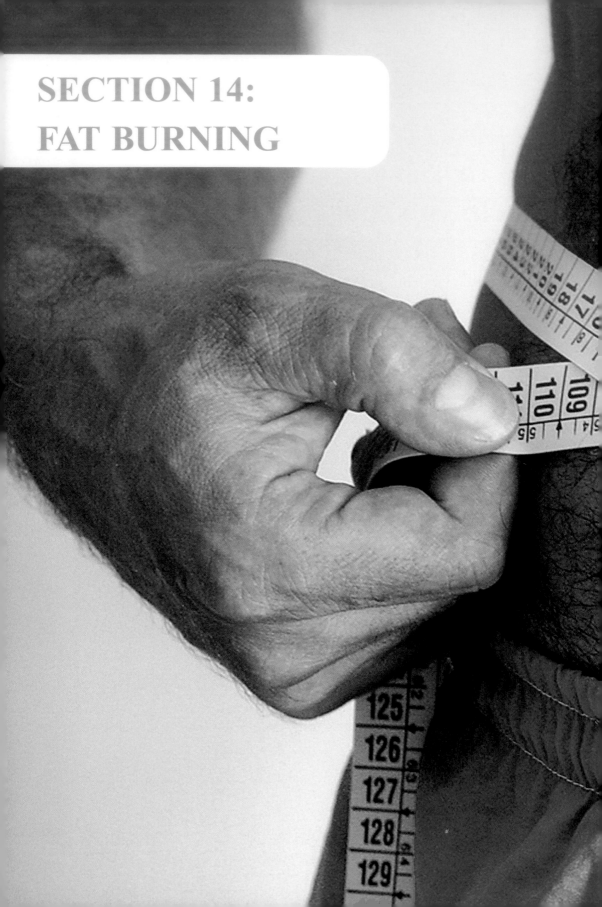

SECTION 14:
FAT BURNING

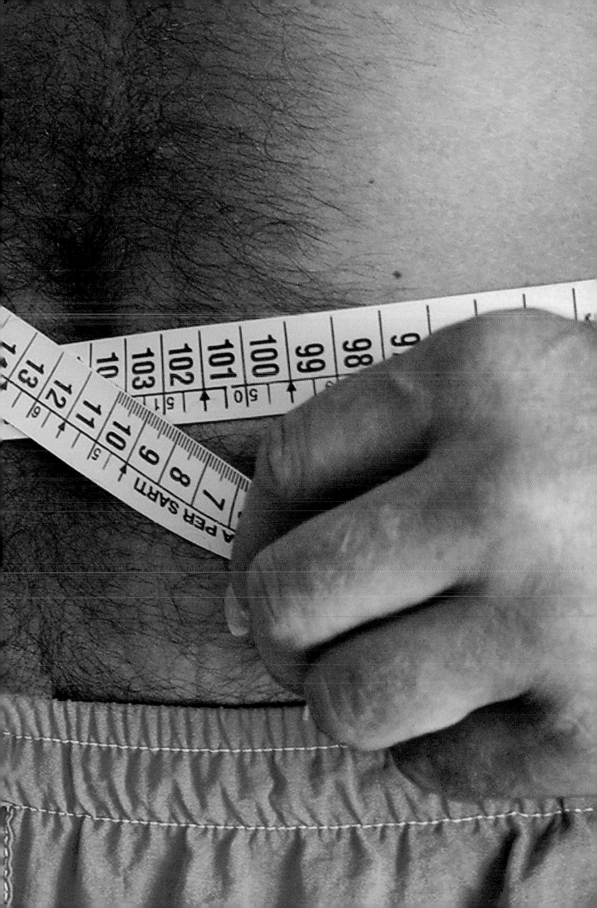

Question

How can I lose weight during a marathon training program?

Answer

When runners try to lose significant weight during a marathon training program they often don't get the nutrients needed to keep pushing back the endurance threshold toward the marathon. A modest weight loss of 3-5 pounds is possible without significant nutritional risk when using a good nutritional website, and when replenishing carbohydrates immediately after hard workouts. A great resource (even for men) is A WOMAN'S GUIDE TO FATBURNING & RUNNING – A YEAR ROUND PLAN.

Websites such as

www.fitday.com

can help you control the calorie content. As you log in each day, you'll see whether you are missing key nutrients, and can budget the number of calories consumed. A calorie deficit (more calories burned than consumed) of 75-125 per day has allowed many e-coach clients I've worked with to lose 3-5 pounds.

Question
What and when should I eat immediately after long runs and speed workouts?

Answer

Prime time for replacing the limited glycogen supply in your body is the half hour after finishing the workout. If you are trying to lose weight, eating the snack after the run is crucial for sustained muscle performance – especially on the next run. The best composition of this meal would be 80% simple carbohydrate and 20% protein, according to research. Usually 200-300 calories is sufficient. Glycogen is the stored form of carbohydrate and is the fuel source used during the first 15 minutes of running. Restocked muscles give you more bounce – especially at the beginning of your next run.

Question

Why would I gain weight during a marathon training program?

Answer

Several physiological changes occur as you increase the length of your long runs.

1. Blood volume increases.

2. The amount of glycogen stored in the muscles increases.

3. For every gram of glycogen, four grams of water are stored nearby.

Most marathoners can expect a 3-7 pound gain from these changes, which allow the muscles to work better. So this weight gain actually helps you run farther and faster. Those who gain more than this range often are mistaken in thinking that when training for a marathon they can eat almost anything they want. In practice, this will cause a weight gain due to more calories on the income side of the ledger.

Question

How does marathon training help you burn fat?

Answer

You don't maximize fat burning until you have been running for more than 45 minutes, and only if you are going slowly enough. Liberal walk breaks help you stay in the fat burning zone. By running at least three sessions a week longer than 45 minutes, with one more than 90 minutes, your muscle cells can adapt to more efficient fat-burning, because there is little waste product. Running also raises the core body temperature which when done regularly for a sustained workout may trigger a lower set amount of fat on the body.

Question
How do I know if I'm getting enough nutrients?

Answer

It helps to use a website such as www.fitday.com. You can receive a daily report on each of the recommended nutrients, and then take action if you are low on any of them.

Question
Are there some other exercises that can help me burn more fat?

Answer

Walking is probably the best exercise to increase the quantity of fat burning. By increasing the daily number of segments of 100-500 steps, during the periods of the day when you are waiting for something (meetings, kids, planes), you can significantly increase the number of calories burned per week. In addition, cross-training modes such as Nordic track, rowing machines, elliptical, etc., can add calories burned on non-running days.

SECTION 15:
RECOVERY

Question
What should I do right after the race?

Answer

1. Keep walking for at least half a mile (1 km). This will continue the pumping action of the muscles, removing waste products and circulating fresh blood.

2. Eat a 200-300 calorie snack containing 80% simple carbohydrate and 20% protein within 30 minutes of finishing. If you cannot get protein, eat simple carbohydrate.

3. Later in the afternoon, walk around gently for another 30-60 minutes.

Question
Does a cold bath really help recovery?

Answer

I've talked to hundreds of runners who have experienced significantly faster recovery after soaking in cool water during the two hour period past the finish line. Simply submerge your legs in a tub of water for at least 15 minutes. The temperature of the water needs to be 20 degrees cooler than body temperature. I believe that ice is not necessary if the water temperature is 78°F (25°C) or cooler.

Question

Does wearing a compression sleeve speed up recovery?

Answer

Experts believe that compression sleeves around the calf muscle, such as the Zensah sleeve, can help the muscle cells return blood flow to the heart. Experts advise that if you are sitting in a car or plane after a marathon, there is a slight increase in blood clot risk, which is reduced by wearing these compression devices. I recommend using the Zensah product.

Question

How much should I run the week after a "to finish" marathon?

Answer

The day after the marathon, I recommend walking at least 30 minutes, but 45 minutes is better. Two days after the race you can walk for 45 minutes with some 10-60 second jog segments, every minute or two. For the next week, alternate walking one day, and walking with run breaks the next, gradually increasing the running portion while decreasing the walk segment. Most of my runners are back to "normal" runs within 2-3 weeks.

Question
How soon can I run fast after a marathon?

Answer

It's best to wait at least 3 weeks before running a race, a speed workout or anything that is faster than a jog or slow running pace. Even if you feel like doing so, it is best to stay slow. The lingering fatigue in a muscle can lead to an overuse injury without warning.

Question

How soon can I run another marathon?

Answer

If you have paced yourself correctly and taken the appropriate run-walk-run ratio, the following recovery period applies:

If you ran 2 or more minutes per mile slower than you could have run on that day, most can run another marathon within 3-4 weeks. There is no need to do a long run in this case because the previous marathon provided the endurance needed.

If you ran 1 to 1.5 min/mi slower than you could have run in an all-out marathon race, and there are no extraordinary damage signs, most can run another marathon 6-8 weeks after the first one. In this case, one needs a long run of 26 miles, 3-4 weeks before your next one and 3-4 weeks after the first one.

If the first marathon was run at top capacity, then it's best to wait 4-6 months before attempting another marathon. The long runs would need to build back to 26-29 miles, 3-4 weeks before the next marathon.

Note:

For more information, see my book RUNNING – A YEAR ROUND PLAN.

Question

Is there a newsletter that will keep me informed of updates to the information in this book?

Answer

Yes, my e-newsletter is free. Register at

www.JeffGalloway.com

Question

What are the other Galloway Books?

Answer

- Half-Marathon – You Can Do It
- Galloway's 5K/10K Running
- Running – Getting Started
- Women's Complete Guide to Running
- Women's Complete Guide to Walking
- Running and Fatburning for Women
- Running – Testing Yourself
- Running Until You're 100
- Running – A Year Round Plan
- Walking – The Complete Book
- Fit Kids – Smarter Kids

Photo & Illustration Credits

Fotolia.com:

p.6-7 sportgraphic; p.8 Alex Kalmbach; p.13 Marcel Mooij; p.15 Galina Barskaya; p.17 Dimitar Marino;, p.20-21 Amridesign; p.26-27; p. 86 AwD; p.32 Pablo Viñas; p.34 Philip Lange; p.38-39 Wojciech Gajda; p. 46, p. 104 Elisabeth Pérotin; p.47 Kati Molin; p.48 Jens Hilberger; p.55 Elisabeth Pérotin; p.60-61 Liv Friis-larsen; p.63 fooddesign; p.64 Torsten Schon; p.68-69 Eric Gevaert, p.71 Accent; p.84-85 Saniphoto; p.92 Christopher Nuzzaco; p.96-97 allievn; p.108-109 danielschoenen; p.116 robynmac; p.118 photoL, p.121 Rafa Irusta Machin; p.124 Eric Gevaert; p.133 Okea; p.136-137 Roman Safreider; p.138 Bernd_Leitner; p.140 - 141 Philip Lange; p.142 Eric Gevaert; p.145 Stefan Redel www.stefanredel.de; p.146 Irene Stühmeier; p.147 dean sanderson; p.152 Andy Dean; p.160 Marina Bartel; p.165 Stephen Coburn; p.166 Mark Atkins; p.169 PeJo; p.170-171 ernard BAILLY; p.172 Elisabeth Pérotin; p.178 - 179; p.181 www.dinostock.com; p.186-187 soschoenbistdu; p.189 4uphoto; p.197 r-o-x-o-r

All other photos: Mizuno

Cover photo: dpa Picture-Alliance GmbH

Cover design: Jens Vogelsang

Jeff Galloway

ISBN: 978-1-84126-218-5
$ 16.95 US
£ 12.95 / € 16.95

ISBN: 978-1-84126-219-2
$ 16.95 US
£ 12.95 / € 16.95

ISBN: 978-1-84126-205-5
$ 16.95 US
£ 12.95 / € 16.95

ISBN: 978-1-84126-243-7
$ 17.95 US
£ 14.95 / € 16.95

ISBN: 978-1-84126-242-0
$ 16.95 US
£ 12.95 / € 16.95

MEYER
& MEYER
SPORT

www.m-m-sports.com